Go Ahead, Make My Drink

60 RECIPES
Inspired by the Best of Film and Television

TEXT BY **ANTHONY MARINESE** ILLUSTRATIONS BY **HORACIO CASSINELLI**

INSIGHT 👁 EDITIONS

San Rafael, California

CONTENTS

The Classics

Some New Classics

Introduction

Alcohol and pop culture have been among the most influential aspects of civilization since well before the Romans were watching gladiators and drinking wine in the Coliseum. People have always had a desire for inebriation and a need to be entertained. Before cocktails, it was beer or wine. Before movies or TV, it was stage acting or live performances. These two things are constant and always will be. When the idea for this book was presented to me, it seemed like such a natural and necessary combination. I was surprised it hadn't been done before. I've been a bartender for a long time now, and one of the only things I like more than a nice balanced cocktail is a good movie. Much of my life has been influenced by pop culture and making cocktails. I know that I am not alone in this. You are reading this book because you obviously share my interests here. I put a lot of care and work into this book. It was definitely a labor of love. I wanted to make another way for you to be able to connect with and enjoy some of the most iconic things in pop culture.

With as much love as I put into this book, I needed the perfect artist to visually convey these ideas and references. Horacio definitely lived up to my expectations. Above and beyond. I am so happy that we were able to come together for this project, and I know that there is no other artist who could have done it better. So please enjoy our book. Use it, share it, but most of all, have fun with it. After all, isn't that the point? So it is with much excitement and a bit of nervousness that we proudly present to you: *Go Ahead, Make My Drink*. Cheers!

To alcohol!
The cause of, and solution to,
all of life's problems.

—HOMER SIMPSON

A Few Notes on Technique

None of the drinks in this book are very difficult to make. Some of the recipes simply take more time or preparation; that's all. With the right tools, the right ingredients, a little patience, and some technique, you will see that all of the drinks in these pages are relatively easy to pull off successfully. This is the section where I give you, the reader, some tips, some explanations, and some lessons on the basics of drink mixing.

∗ SHAKE AND STRAIN ∗

This is putting your chosen ingredients into a mixing glass and placing the metal end of your Boston shaker over the top of the glass. Tap the metal part on the end to ensure that the fit on the glass is nice and tight. Shake with both hands, one on each of the two parts of the shaker. It is important to remember: Always shake your drink with glass end up. Shake it vigorously for about ten to fifteen seconds. Tap the side of the shaker with the heel of your hand until it loosens itself. Separate the two so that the drink is in the clear mixing glass. Put your strainer on the top of the glass and pour into your chosen glassware. This serves a few purposes: It not only makes everything cold and mixes everything very nicely, but it also melts some of the ice so your drink gets watered down a bit and becomes more palatable.

∗ STIR AND STRAIN ∗

For this you need a clear pint glass or a mixing glass and a barspoon. Pour your ingredients into the glass and add some ice cubes, not crushed. We use the cubes so there isn't too much watering down, but just enough. Put your barspoon into the glass. Touching the inside of the glass, move the spoon all the way to the bottom of whatever you are mixing. Stir fast but gently, touching your barspoon along the glass all the time as you are stirring. We want it all to stir at the same time but not add unneeded air into the drink, so keep the spoon pretty close to the bottom of the glass while stirring. The best way is to try to hold the spoon in your fingers in such a way that, while stirring, the back of the spoon is always touching the glass, so you are turning the spoon in your fingers while stirring. Not totally necessary, but something to practice.

∗ D R Y   S H A K I N G ∗

When you are making a drink with cream or egg white, you want it to be frothy. The best way for this is when you are making your drink, first put the egg white, or cream, or both, and sugar or simple syrup, if needed, into a shaker. Make sure the shaker you are using has a very firm seal. If not, you can get a leak, and this method can easily turn into a mess. Shake them all together with no ice. The longer and harder you shake them, the better texture your drink will have in the end. After your dry shake, add the rest of your ingredients and the ice. Shake it all again for just a little more time than you think you should. The point of drinks like these is the texture, and this is how you get it right.

∗ F L O A T I N G ∗

Floating is when you keep your ingredients mostly in separate layers in the same glass. The easiest way to do this is with the help of your barspoon. Pour in the glass first the bottom layer of your drink. Afterwards, place the bowl of your barspoon on top of the drink, so it is touching the bottom layer but not totally submerged. Pour the ingredient you want to float very slowly onto the spoon. Gently remove the spoon and you should have a separated layer. It takes practice, but once you get it, it is pretty easy.

∗ M U D D L I N G ∗

For some drinks, you need to smash some of your ingredients with a blunt object. This is your muddler. Usually made of wood, they are long, thin, and solid, with a flattened, slightly round end. How hard you muddle depends on what you are smashing. Things you need the juice from—like fruit—you have to use your muddler to really smash them good. But for more delicate things, like leaves, as in the mint leaves in a mojito, you only lightly press on them to extract the oils from their veins. If you smash them too much, it will make the drink bitter.

∗ F L A V O R E D   S Y R U P S ∗

Making flavored syrups is an easy way to impress your guests and to make a unique flavor for anything you like. In a saucepan, add equal parts, in weight, of white granulated sugar and water. Chop finely whatever you are trying to extract the flavor from. Some examples are chilies, fruit peels, herbs, or whatever else you like. Prepare enough so that the combination of all the additional ingredients is equal in weight to the portions of sugar or water used. Combine everything before the syrup is heated. Let everything heat up slowly and simmer together on a low heat for fifteen minutes or so and taste it along the way until it's to your liking. It is important to simmer on a low heat and be continuously stirring it, because if it gets too hot or still for too long, you might caramelize the sugar and ruin the syrup. After it is ready, remove any solid pieces by pouring it through a fine cocktail strainer into whatever container you have ready for it. Remember, the longer you cook it, the thicker it will get. That can be good or bad, depending on what you are using it for. If you flavor your syrup with fresh ingredients, it's got a shelf life of about three weeks at room temperature or five weeks if kept cold.

✳ B L E N D I N G ✳

Some of the recipes in this book require the use of an electric blender. Something to keep in mind is that alcohol makes ice melt faster, so of all the ingredients going into the blender, make the alcohol the last thing you add. Once you have everything in the blender, turn it on, and blend until it is smooth but not totally liquid. It should be smooth enough to pour out of the blender and into the glassware you are planning to use.

✳ R O L L I N G ✳

When a drink needs to be mixed but not a lot, you need only to "roll" it. This is the case for a few of the thicker drinks, such as a Bloody Mary or the Atlanta Zombie. Rolling a drink is when you carefully pour all of the ingredients from one glass to another. This will mix your ingredients perfectly enough for the drinks that call for this method.

✳ H E A T I N G   O R   C H I L L I N G   A   G L A S S / B O W L ✳

When you are making a warm drink, it is necessary to have a warm cup to pour it into, just as it is necessary to pour cold drinks into a cold glass. To heat a glass, let it sit for a few minutes full of hot water. Dump the water right before replacing it with your hot cocktail. To chill a glass, fill it with cold water and ice while you prepare the drink and dump out the cold water as a last step before pouring the cold cocktail into the glass.

✳ T H E   B I G   I C E   C U B E ✳

Drinking a cocktail in a short wide, clear glass over one big ice cube is a beautiful thing. It looks great, it feels great, and best of all, it keeps your drink cold without melting too fast and watering down your cocktail before you can finish it. Most home furnishing stores will sell the mold for making bigger cubes, or you can find them online. If you can't get your hands on a big ice cube mold, you can find or make a container the size of the cube you want, fill it with water, and freeze it. For those of you who are really into details and presentation, if you boil the water before you fill the ice cube mold, your cubes will come out clear with no cloudy appearance. Not necessary but definitely a cool touch.

THE RIGHT TOOLS FOR THE JOB

Bartenders are craftsmen. We create drinks for the enjoyment of others, which in turn brings us joy as well. Like any other craftsman, the bartender needs a specific set of tools for the job at hand. Most of the tools needed can be found at any cookware store, or if you can't find it exactly, there is always room for improvisation. As long as you know the purpose for the tool you need, you can find something similar in your kitchen or around your house to use in its place. Remember to wash whatever you use before you use it.

✳ THE BARSPOON ✳

The barspoon is one of your more important pieces. They are long, thin, and twisted in the middle. The barspoon is a must-have tool for making any drink that requires stirring. The thin shape and small bowl are perfect for the job at hand, and the twist down the middle makes possible the stirring motion you need. Also, the small bowl is a great tool for measuring a very small amount of something in your drink.

✳ THE SHAKER ✳

There are two types of shakers most commonly used. I prefer the Boston shaker. It consists of two pieces. Both pieces are in the shape of a drinking glass. One side is metal and slightly bigger. The other half is the same shape but smaller, so it can fit into the larger half. The small half can be glass or metal. The other type of shaker is a three piece, with a top that has a built-in strainer. Either type will get the job done, but the Boston shaker gets a tighter seal. In the end, it's just about personal preference.

* THE MUDDLER *

This is the long, thin, solid blunt object used for smashing ingredients to extract their desired properties. If it is juice from a lime, crushed sugar, or the oil from a mint leaf, it's all in how you use your muddler. Muddlers can be made of various types of metal, plastic, or wood as well.

* THE STRAINER *

There are two types of strainers used most often by bartenders. The Hawthorne strainer is most commonly seen. It has a handle and a flat round perforated head, with a spring coiled along the edge of it. It is used for any drink that you shake and strain. The other is called a julep strainer. It also has a handle, but the head is slightly concave, and takes more of an oval shape. It is used in any drink that called for you to stir and strain it.

∗ THE JIGGERS ∗

These are the fast and easy-to-use tools for quickly measuring small amounts of liquid. They are almost always two sided, with each side being a different measurement. For example, one side could be ¾ ounce, and the other could be 1 ounce—or any other combination, the smallest being ¼ ounce and the biggest jigger you will be able to find will probably be 2 ounces. They are wide at the openings and narrow in the middle to make holding them and dumping them much faster and easier.

∗ PROPER GLASSWARE ∗

Using the right glass for a cocktail does indeed serve a purpose. It could be for maintaining the temperature of your drink for longer, or for the presentation, or even for just making your drink easier to walk around with. Having your drink in the proper glass is important but, at the same time, not crucial. When I spend time and energy on making a cocktail, I feel it needs a worthy vessel . . . But, then again, if you want to drink your martini from a whiskey glass, go for it. It's your drink!

The Classics

—————————————————— * ——————————————————

The following section contains the libations of choice for some of pop culture's most iconic characters. These are classic, time-tested recipes of drinks made in the fashion that their inventors intended. Some of these recipes were created by great bartenders of the past, and some were from the mind of the person who created the character who drinks it. Most of these drinks are very tasty. A few, though, were created only for their novelty value. It is pretty easy to tell the difference. That being said, everyone has a different preference, so if the recipe for any drink sounds like something you might like—novelty or not—then please, by all means, make it and try it out. Drinking the same thing as your favorite character while watching them drink it is a great way to feel more like a part of whatever it is you're watching. It is a way to experience a movie or TV show with not only the sights and sounds, but also taste, texture, and buzz of the alcohol that the characters you are watching are feeling in that same moment. For a lover of pop culture, this can be a very magical thing.

THE BIG BANG THEORY

Grasshopper

1 ounce green crème de menthe
1 ounce white crème de cocoa
1 ounce cream

Combine all ingredients in
a shaker with ice. Shake
vigorously and strain into a
chilled martini glass.

The very nerdy astrophysicist
Dr. Raj Koothrappali has a blind
date with family friend, Lalita
Gupta. Only one problem: He has
"selective mutism" and cannot
speak in front of women. Luckily
for him, Penny just got offered
a few bartending shifts at The
Cheesecake Factory and needs
to practice her drink making.
After serving Raj a grasshopper,
he immediately starts talking
to Penny, and we all learn that
drinking alcohol seems to
cure Raj's disorder. He exclaims
drunkenly to Penny, "I need to have a Lupita
before I meet the grasshopper!"

Raj drinks too much on the date and becomes
obnoxious, and Sheldon unknowingly steals
his date by telling her she looks like a fictional
princess from a story. BAZINGA!

THE BIG LEBOWSKI

White Russian

6 ounces vodka
1 ounce coffee liqueur
1 ounce of cream

Combine all ingredients in
a shaker, add ice and shake.
Strain into a glass of at least
8 ounces or more filled with
ice cubes.

Jeff Lebowski is one of the most loved characters Jeff Bridges ever played. More commonly known as "the dude, or his dudeness, duder, or el dudarino, if, you know, you're not into that whole brevity thing," the Dude is the lead character in the Coen brothers' cult classic *The Big Lebowski*. He is an unemployed, pot smoking slacker, who happens to share a name with a millionaire. After a case of mistaken identity, the Dude feels that the other Lebowski, the "big" Lebowski, owes him a new rug. One more thing, the Dude loves his White Russians. The White Russian is a drink that has been around for a while. It's sweet and creamy, and strong, and very delicious. More than one scene shows him drinking or mixing one. He is such a fan of White Russians, that in one scene, where he has no cream, he uses powdered creamer instead. White Russians are as big a part of this film as bowling, or nihilists, or the Dude's piss soaked rug (which really pulled the room together). This movie can be credited with a renewed interest in this almost forgotten drink, and no Lebowski party is complete without a few White Russians going around.

GUYS AND DOLLS

Milk Punch

2 ounces white rum
¼ ounce dark rum
½ ounce simple syrup
4 ounces whole milk
A few drops of vanilla extract

Shake all the ingredients together with ice. Strain into a tall glass with ice or into an empty coconut shell if you've got one handy. Grate some nutmeg on top for garnish.

Frank Sinatra plays Nathan Detroit. He is a small-time criminal in New York City. He needs some money for setting up some illegal craps games with other older gangsters. In order to get this money, he has made a big money bet with notorious gambler Sky Masterson, played by Marlon Brando. Detroit bets Masterson $1,000 that Masterson can't get a girl of Detroit's choosing to go on a date with him in Havana, Cuba. Masterson accepts the challenge, and Detroit chooses the very strict, straight-laced "church lady," Sgt. Sarah Brown (Jean Simmons), sister of the Save-a-Soul Mission, religious devotee, and non-drinker. After promising Sarah Brown more attendance at her Sunday service, she agrees to the date. Masterson takes her to Havana, and gets her drunk by ordering them milk punch, and telling her that they contain a milk preservative called "Bacardi." This movie was made in 1955, five years before the Cuban Revolution. Bacardi was still made in Cuba then but moved to Puerto Rico during the revolution. Sky Masterson and the church lady both eventually fall in love with each other, and he tells her it started as a bet, and she is eventually fine with it.

THE BLUES BROTHERS

Orange Whip

1 ounce light rum
1 ounce vodka
4 ounces orange juice
Splash of cream

Pour all ingredients into a shaker with ice, shake and strain into a Collins class filled with ice cubes. Garnish with a slice of orange.

Jake and Elwood Blues (John Belushi and Dan Aykroyd) are fresh out of jail and on the run! They are "on a mission from God" to raise money to save the orphanage they grew up in. Unless the orphanage can pay $5,000 in back taxes it will be closed forever.

Don't worry; Jake and Elwood have a plan. To get the money, they organize a big, fund raising concert.

This movie is full of legends of blues and soul music: Ray Charles, Aretha Franklin, James Brown, Cab Calloway, just to name a few. Jake's parole officer Burton Mercer (John Candy) shows up to the concert to arrest them for causing mayhem all over Chicago. Mercer decides that before he makes his arrest, he wants to enjoy some of the concert with his fellow officers and orders everyone a round of Orange Whips. "Who wants an Orange Whip? Orange Whip? Orange Whip? Three Orange Whips!"

CASABLANCA

French 75

1 ounce gin
½ ounce lemon juice
¼ ounce simple syrup
2 ounces champagne

Combine all ingredients in a champagne flute of 5 ounces or more. Add the champagne last and gently.

After being rejected by Rick (Humphrey Bogart), Yvonne (Madeleine LeBeau) shows up at his bar, Rick's American Café, with a German officer she is now interested in. She orders a round of French 75s from the strange Russian bartender. The French 75 is a cocktail named after the French-made 75 mm. cannons used to fight the Germans in WWI. It makes you wonder if the German officer drinking the French 75 in this scene can appreciate the irony of the situation. The French 75 cocktail as we see it here is the currently accepted recipe. This drink has been made a few different ways in its lifetime, but this is the recipe as it is made now. This drink is very delicious and goes perfectly with this movie. *Casablanca* is one of those films that everyone needs to see at least once. It is a classic story with some of the silver screen's most iconic players. Now "round up the usual suspects" and make some French 75s for yourselves. Here's looking at you, kid.

Manhattan

2 ½ ounces bourbon
1 ¼ ounces sweet vermouth
2 dashes of angostura bitters

In a mixing glass, add all ingredients and ice. Stir and strain into a chilled martini glass and garnish with a maraschino cherry. Or an orange peel. It's better with the orange peel.

After witnessing a mob murder (the famous 1929 St. Valentine's Day Massacre in Chicago), two men, Joe and Jerry, dress as women and go on the run in the cargo car of a train headed to sunny Florida. In the same car as Joe and Jerry is an all-girl band led by the singer, Sugar Kane (Marilyn Monroe). Jerry likes Sugar and is about to reveal his identity to her when the girls realize they have all the ingredients for Manhattans. A cocktail party breaks out, and while Sugar is chipping ice with a drumstick, another girl is shaking the cocktail in a hot water bottle. I suggest to stir this cocktail and to use a proper cold glass unless it's Prohibition Era in the United States, alcohol has been made illegal, you're hiding on a train in the cargo hold, and paper cups are all you've got available. In that case, you can't be too picky.

Hot Toddy

1 ½ ounces whiskey
1 tablespoon of honey
¼ ounce lemon juice
6 ounces or so of boiling water
4 to 6 whole cloves

In a preheated glass of 8 ounces or more, add the lemon juice, whiskey, and honey. Mix them all thoroughly in the glass and add the water last so that it will not lose heat from the mixing of the ingredients. Garnish with a few cloves and a lemon peel. Serve hot.

This 1958 movie, starring Elizabeth Taylor and Paul Newman, was adapted for the screen from a play by Tennessee Williams. The play is considered one of the best classic American plays, and Williams even won a Pulitzer Prize in Drama for it in 1955. In the story, our main character, Brick (Newman), is an aging ex-athlete and heir to a cotton plantation. Brick is also a heavy drinker. We learn later in the story that Brick's best friend Skipper has killed himself, and this is what has led to Brick's alcoholism. Anyhow, Brick gets drunk one night and breaks his leg while trying to prove he is still an athlete. Brick and his wife Maggie (Taylor) leave the next day to visit Brick's family's plantation for Big Daddy's birthday. We find out later that Big Daddy is dying, but the doctors didn't tell him. Also, we learn that Maggie was always jealous of Brick and Skipper's relationship, and she accuses the two of being lovers and then lies to Brick's terminally ill father about being pregnant. Poor Brick! If I was him, I'd be drinking too! One of Brick's many favorite drinks is the Hot Toddy. This is a very old drink with conflicting origin stories, as is usually the case with old recipes. Nowadays Hot Toddies are most commonly made with lemon, honey, whiskey, cloves, and hot water. They are either drunk when it's cold outside or when someone is sick. Victoria Moore describes them as "vitamin C for health, honey to soothe, and alcohol to numb." This is also one of those recipes where everyone likes theirs a little different. People will add spices, or tea, or cider, or anything else that they think will taste good, so feel free to experiment and make it to your taste. Just remember: It's hot and has whiskey or brandy, honey, and citrus. Beyond that, it's really up to you.

Red Eye

1 ounce vodka
4 ounces tomato juice
1 bottle of beer
1 raw egg

In a large, wide-mouth glass, pour the vodka and tomato juice into the glass. Crack the egg and pour its contents into the glass as well. Do not stir the drink. Open a can of beer and put the whole can open and upside down into the glass, so that the beer is slowly leaking out into the rest of the drink. Enjoy . . . ?

"Hey, bartender, you know how to make a Red Eye?" *Cocktail* is a movie about a new young bartender, Brian (Tom Cruise), who has started bartending to make some cash after business school. Brian learns some life lessons from his new bartending and flair mentor, Doug Coughlin (Bryan Brown). The Red Eye is meant to be a hangover cure. I have no evidence to back up that statement, so don't depend on this drink as the remedy to your hangover. But also I know that there are a few other supposed hangover cures that involve these or similar ingredients, or something similar, so maybe there is something to it. I say that if you can stomach drinking this, I think you're going to be OK.

Mojito

5 to 7 fresh mint leaves
1 ½ ounces white rum
¾ ounce simple syrup
¾ ounce fresh lime juice
Splash of soda water

In a tall Collins glass, add the simple syrup, the lime juice, and the mint leaves. Gently muddle the leaves only to break the veins on the leaves, not to shred the whole thing. Add ice and rum. Gently stir and top off with a splash of soda water. Garnish with a slice of lime and some fresh mint.

"I'm a fiend for Mojitos." Sonny Crockett is the white-blazer-wearing Miami police detective in the hit TV series *Miami Vice*. This series was one of the most watched series in the United States from 1984 to 1989. Sonny (Don Johnson) and his partner Rico Tubbs (Philip Michael Thomas) get into car chases, bust up drug deals, and solve murders that were mostly based on real crimes of the time happening in Miami, Florida. The fashion, the action, and the New Wave music are what made the series so iconic. *People* magazine said it was "the first show to look really new and different since the color TV was invented." In 2006, Universal Pictures released a blockbuster-film version starring Colin Farrell and Jamie Foxx as Sonny and Rico. It was a pretty big success, one of director Michael Mann's best. The line where Sonny orders the Mojito is from the movie. Just to be clear—for the fanatics.

BREAKFAST AT TIFFANY'S

White Angel

2 ounces vodka
2 ounces gin

In a mixing glass, add the gin, the vodka, and ice. Stir until ice cold, and strain into a chilled martini glass. No garnish.

This drink, the White Angel, was made up by Joe Bell, the fictional bartender from Truman Capote's 1958 novelette *Breakfast at Tiffany's*. Joe made this drink and gave it to the nameless narrator, asking for his opinion on it while they talk about Mr. Yunioshi seeing Holly Golightly in Africa. This scene is left out of the movie, and so is one of the book's best characters, Joe the bartender. Also in the movie, the narrator gets a name (Paul) and is played by George Peppard. Mickey Rooney does an incredibly racist version of Mr. Yunioshi, and the unforgettable Audrey Hepburn in her most memorable, and iconic, role plays the socialite call girl Holly Golightly. Holly must be something special if Sally Tomato pays her $100 a week to visit him in Sing-Sing prison just for the weather report. Whatever version you prefer, book or movie, this drink goes perfectly with both. Here's to Joe Bell!

DJANGO UNCHAINED

Polynesian Pearl Diver

1 ½ ounces white rum
½ ounce 151-proof Demerara rum
½ ounce dark rum
¾ ounce pearl diver mix
1 teaspoon velvet falernum, a syrup common with tiki drinks
1 ounce orange juice
¾ ounce lime juice

Put all ingredients into a blender. Add ice—5 ounces or so. Blend until smooth. Pour into a coconut or a glass of 8 ounces or more.

PEARL DIVER MIX
To make the pearl diver mix, don't make it for one drink. This is the recipe for about three or four drinks' worth. Scale up the recipe for what you need.

Mix 1 ounce honey, 1 ounce melted butter, ¼ ounce simple syrup, a dash of cinnamon, a dash of vanilla, and a dash of allspice dram (pimento liqueur). Blend all together and refrigerate until it is cold.

Quentin Tarantino's *Django Unchained* is full of some pretty horrible characters. One of the worst is Calvin Candie (Leonardo DiCaprio). His infamous slave plantation, "Candyland," is where we first meet Candie. He is in his bar betting on a forced fight to the death between two slaves. This is where our heroes, Dr. King Shultz (Christoph Waltz) and Django (Jamie Foxx), are introduced to him under the guise of a potential slave buyer and his free black partner. Candie then goes to his bar and orders a drink, "I will have a Polynesian Pearl Diver, and do not spare the rum!" The strange thing is, this drink wasn't invented until about seventy-five years after this movie takes place. It was invented by the one and only Don "the Beachcomber" in Los Angeles sometime in the 1930s. This drink is ordered so clearly and obviously in this scene that it cannot be an accident in the script but is rather a homage to a famous Los Angeles bartender.

THE ROYAL TENENBAUMS

Bloody Mary

2 ounces vodka
4 ounces tomato juice
Dash of pepper
Dash of salt
Dash of Worcestershire sauce
Dash of tobacco
Dash of angostura bitters
Just a small bit of horseradish

Fill a glass of 10 ounces or more
with ice. Add all the ingredients
and pour back and forth between two
glasses a few times to mix thoroughly,
but don't shake the mix too much.

"Dear Eli, I'm in the middle of the ocean. I haven't left my room in four days. I've never been so lonely in my whole life. I think I'm in love with Margot." This movie was co-written by Owen Wilson, but it is definitely in classic Wes Anderson–style: monotone characters, awkward silences, great costumes, and famous actors who probably were in another of his movies as well. All three Tenenbaum kids are weird in their own way, but Richie Tenenbaum is a very strange character. Loosely based on a famous tennis player who retired at a very young age but had the same headband-and-glasses look, Richie (Luke Wilson) is the favorite son of Royal Tenenbaum (Gene Hackman). He is an ex-tennis pro, a talented artist, and an alcoholic. As a child, he had a pet falcon named Mordecai, and he was always painting—mostly pictures of his adopted sister, Margot (Gwyneth Paltrow). As an adult, Richie's tennis career was at its peak until he had a breakdown during a live televised tennis match. Since then, he has been living on a ship, drinking Bloody Marys and traveling the world by sea. In more than one scene in this movie, Richie has a Bloody Mary in his hand. He drinks so many of them that he even carries a bottle of black pepper in his jacket pocket, just in case.

7 and 7

1 ½ ounces Canadian Whiskey
3 ounces lemon-lime flavored soda

This drink is called 7 and 7 because it was made with Seagram's 7 whiskey and 7UP lemon-lime soda. The measurements are not exact, depending on the glass you are using, but basically, use twice the amount of lemon-lime soda as you do whiskey.

The 7 and 7 is the go-to drink for this movie's main character Tony Manero. It is a simple yet strong drink, made so that the drinker doesn't taste the alcohol, just the sweet bubbly mixer. It is very popular still to young drinkers like Tony Manero. John Travolta plays Manero, the nineteen-year-old king of the dance floor at a club called 2001 Odyssey in Brooklyn, New York. Manero lives for Saturday nights. It is his opportunity to be the star instead of on weekdays, when he is a nobody who works in a small hardware store.

Travolta was already known before this movie for his role as Vinnie Barbarino in *Welcome Back, Kotter*, but *Saturday Night Fever* made him a real star. This movie also can claim some of the credit for making disco music so popular. Thanks a lot, *Saturday Night Fever* . . .

THE GREAT GATSBY

Gin Rickey

2 ounces gin
1 half lime
Soda water

Use a glass of 8 ounces or more, fill it with ice, squeeze all of the juice from the lime half, and drop the spent lime. Add the gin and top it off with the soda water. Stir gently with your straw.

Mint Julep

3 ounces bourbon
A full barspoon of sugar
6 or so fresh mint leaves
Crushed ice
One very cold 12-ounce old-fashioned glass or a silver mint julep cup

In the bottom of your cup, drop in the mint leaves and the sugar. Muddle them gently but firmly—enough to break the veins on the leaves but not shred them. Fill half the cup with crushed ice, pour in bourbon, and stir. Fill the cup with more crushed ice, packed in tight. Garnish with a few fresh mint leaves.

There is a lot of drinking going on in *The Great Gatsby*. A lot of different libations are mentioned: champagne cocktails, Mint Juleps, Bronx cocktails, to name a few. I went with the Gin Rickey, because legend has it, this was the favorite of the author, F. Scott Fitzgerald. I also included the Mint Julep, because it is definitely enjoyed in this story, but more important, because it is a cocktail everyone should know how to make. It's easy, classic, and perfect for drinking on a nice warm day in the summer.

This story takes place during a very decadent era of American history—the Roaring Twenties. Alcohol was illegal, but people were drinking more and partying harder than before Prohibition laws passed. The bootleggers (a slang term for transporters and sellers of illegally made or imported alcohol) had a lot of extra cash. The book's title character, Jay Gatsby, started from nothing, came from a poor family, and made his millions from bootlegging. So, of course, his parties would have been very, very drunken occasions.

Thanks-tini

2 ½ ounces potato-based vodka
1 ½ ounces cranberry juice
¼ cube beef bouillon

Shake all ingredients in a
martini glass vigorously. Strain
into a chilled martini glass.

HIMYM, as the fans call it, is a
show about a guy, Ted, who is
telling his kids a nine-year-long
story of how he met their mother.
The show depicts Ted and his
four best friends in New York,
getting into various hilarious
situations. In the 2005 Thanksgiving episode "Belly Full of Turkey," a new drink, the Thanks-tini
is introduced. This is a "fun and
delicious" drink invented by one
of the shows main characters,
Barney Stinson (Neil Patrick Har-
ris), for Thanksgiving. According
to Barney, it is supposed to taste just like a
turkey dinner. Marshall seemed to think, "It's
like Thanksgiving in my mouth!" It is OK . . .
but remember, as Barney said, it is a novelty
drink. Also, I would shake it very well and use
a fine strainer to stop any big pieces of bouillon from getting into the glass.

JACKIE BROWN

Screwdriver

1 ½ ounces vodka
3 ounces orange juice

Fill an 8-ounce glass with ice.
Add the vodka and orange
juice, stir, and drink.

Samuel L. Jackson is the violent,
paranoid, Screwdriver-loving gun
dealer Ordell Robbie in Quentin
Tarantino's *Jackie Brown*. The
legendary Pam Grier, from such
blaxploitation classics as 1973's
Coffy and 1974's *Foxy Brown*, plays
Jackie Brown. Jackie is a flight
attendant who uses her job to
smuggle money into the United
States from Mexico for Ordell
Robbie. This movie was made
as Tarantino's homage to a very
special genre in American cinema:
blaxploitation films. These movies
were popular in the 70s. They were lower
budget B-grade action movies with mostly black
casts, and their target audience was black urban
youth. Most of the films from this genre are now
cult classics. *Shaft*, *Super Fly*, *Blacula*, *Black Belt
Jones*, and one of my favorites, *The Last Dragon*.
Now, in the words of Ordell Robbie himself,
"Do you got some booze? Got some OJ?
Why don't you be a good hostess and hook a
brother up with a Screwdriver?"

JAMES BOND

Vesper Martini

14 ounce Gordon's gin
4 ounces vodka
12 ounces Kina Lillet
One long thin lemon peel

In a shaker add ice, gin, vodka, and Lillet. Shake and strain into a chilled martini glass, garnish with a lemon peel.

In Ian Fleming's 1953 novel *Casino Royale*, James Bond orders this drink of his own invention "shaken until ice cold." The classic Bond line, "shaken, not stirred" wasn't first used until *Diamonds Are Forever*. Bond never said it until *Dr. No*, and Sean Connery said it for the first time as James Bond in *Goldfinger*.

Anyway, in *Casino Royale*, 007 mentions how this drink is nameless, and how he will patent it when he can think of a name. Bond later names the drink after his new love, Vesper Lynd. He falls for Lynd so hard that he contemplates an early retirement from British secret service. In the book, Vesper commits suicide, after guilt of having a husband in the RAF, being a forced double agent, and realizing that she can never escape her past. In the third, (and best), film adaptation of the book in 2006, Vesper dies when she is locked in an elevator in a sinking Venetian building. Whatever the cause of Vesper's death, Bond never orders this drink again. This drink has now become legendary, even though it was only featured in *Casino Royale*, and never after. That is a testament to how delicious the recipe is, and how iconic of a character James Bond has become.

KILL BILL: VOL. 1

Warm Sake

This is not so much a cocktail as it is proper technique for warming and drinking sake.

First, you should get a set of sake cups (*ochoko*), which usually come with a sake jar (*tokkuri*). Never boil or microwave your sake. Instead, fill a pot with hot water to about 98 degrees C. Fill your tokkuri with sake and place it in the water. Let the tokkuri sit in the hot water until it is hot enough for you. The different temperatures have different effects on the flavor and texture of the sake. Try it at every temperature to find what you like. Fifty degrees is considered *joukan* (hot), forty degrees is called *nurukan* (warm), and room temperature sake is called *jouon*. Pour sake into the small cups of your guests first. Pour your own cup last and enjoy in small sips.

"Warm sake? . . . VERY GOOD!" *Itamae* (sushi chef) and legendary sword maker Hattori Hanzo (Sonny Chiba) is the man from Okinawa. When The Bride (Uma Thurman) has "big rats" to kill, she needs a very special sword. The only problem is Hattori Hanzo has made a blood oath to never again make something that kills people. She eventually manages to convince Hanzo to make her a sword she can use to kill Bill, and it is his "greatest creation." This scene begins when The Bride goes to Hanzo's small sushi bar in Okinawa and orders warm sake. When his assistant questions her ordering sake in the middle of the day, Hanzo yells at him: "Day, night, afternoon—who gives a damn?! Get the sake!" The whole time, Hanzo and his assistant do not know that The Bride speaks Japanese and really has no interest in sake, but rather in Japanese steel.

Singapore Sling and a shot of Mescal

1 ounce dry gin
1 ounce cherry heering
1 ounce Benedictine
1 ounce lime juice
2 ounces soda water
1 dash of angostura bitters

Combine gin, Benedictine, lime juice, and cherry heering in a Collins glass filled with ice cubes. Top with soda water and a dash of bitters at the end. Garnish with a cherry. The shot of mescal on the side is just 1 to 2 ounces of mescal in a shot glass.

This Hunter S. Thompson classic first appeared as a two-part story in *Rolling Stone* magazine. It was the first of a style of writing dubbed "gonzo journalism," which is to say that it is part autobiographical fact and part fiction, and it is often very difficult to determine which is which. In the movie, Thompson is portrayed as Raoul Duke (Johnny Depp) and his attorney, Dr. Gonzo, is played by Benicio Del Toro. The two go on a trip to Las Vegas and order this drink combination while in the Pogo Lounge at the Beverly Heights Hotel. This is a movie about two guys who try every drug they can get in excess and destroy every room they step into. It's a crazy spectacle to watch but very entertaining after all. This drink is a powerful combination but not enough to make you see lizard people or try to use a fly swatter to hit swarming bats (unless you're in "bat country"). That effect requires more than alcohol. This drink was originally mixed by Ngiam Tong Boon at the Raffles Hotel in Singapore in the beginning of the twentieth century. The mescal is a distilled spirit made from agave plants in Mexico. It's the name for the family of spirits that tequila belongs to. It's like tequila but not exactly the same.

MAD MEN

Old Fashioned

2 ounces bourbon
2 splashes of soda water
1 sugar cube
2 dashes of angostura bitters
2 orange slices
2 maraschino cherries

In a short, wide whiskey or
old-fashioned glass put one
slice of orange, one cherry,
one splash of soda water,
and the sugar cube. Muddle all together.
When the sugar is mixed in and the fruit is
smashed, take out the spent fruit and add
the bourbon. Stir and add one big ice cube.
Top with the other splash of soda water
and drop into the drink the other piece of
orange and the other cherry.

Jon Hamm is Don Draper.
(Or so he says.) He is the perfect
1960s American version of
masculinity and success. He is
smooth talking, wealthy, well
dressed, good with women, and
almost always orders an Old
Fashioned at the bar. Or at home.
Or anywhere else. Besides a
cigarette, it is the most common
thing in his hand. Draper is the
best of the "Mad Men," slang for
the men in advertising working
on Madison Avenue in New York.
This show is very well regarded
for its historical accuracy to the feelings,
atmosphere, and style of the United States
in this era. The Old Fashioned is THE classic
cocktail. Originally it was bourbon, water, sugar,
and bitters. Maybe a lemon peel. The fruit was
added later for flavor. Every bartender should
know this drink. It is a go-to for anyone looking
for a nice stiff cocktail or who has a taste for
the classics. Now, in Don's words, "Stop talking
and make something of yourself."

MOULIN ROUGE

Absinthe, the classic French way

1 ounce absinthe
3 ounces ice cold water
1 sugar cube

In a clear, fluted glass with a short stem and a wide mouth (a Pontarlier glass if you've got one), pour the absinthe into the glass. Lay a flat, slotted absinthe spoon on the top of the glass and place the sugar cube on top. Slowly drip the cold water on the sugar cube, so that it drips into the absinthe. When the sugar is dissolved, continue dripping in water until all 3 ounces are gone. Stir with the absinthe spoon and enjoy!

It is Paris at the turn of the twentieth century. Montmartre is full of various bohemian characters, and the terminally ill Satine (Nicole Kidman) is the star of the Moulin Rouge. One such character is an English poet named Christian (Ewan McGregor), who falls madly in love with the doomed starlet.

In the opening scene, the small tour of Montmartre takes you past "Bar Absinthe," and Christian asks for his first absinthe almost as soon as he enters the Moulin Rouge. Absinthe was most likely what everyone in the club was drinking. It had the dangerous combination of being both very potent and very delicious. Also, when Christian starts to type in the beginning of the movie, his typewriter is surrounded by half-full glasses of absinthe and various bottles. This is a pretty accurate depiction. The bohemians loved their green fairy, and at that moment in time, the people of France were drinking about 2 million liters of it a year. Within ten more years, it would climb to 36 million liters a year before eventually becoming illegal in 1915. Absinthe was legalized again in most of Europe by the late 1980s.

GODFATHER 2

Banana Daiquiri

1 ½ ounces white rum
½ ounce simple syrup
½ of a banana
½ ounce fresh lime juice

Fill the glass you plan to use with ice to measure how much you need and dump it in a blender. Add all other ingredients and blend until smooth. Pour back into the glass.

Michael Corleone takes over the Corleone crime family when his father Vito retires. He and his older brother, Fredo, are in Havana, Cuba. They are having lunch outside when Fredo gets a taste for Banana Daiquiris and orders multiple rounds of them from the Cuban waiter. At one point, he asks Michael, "How do you say Banana Daiquiri in Spanish?" Fredo is later shot on a boat on Lake Tahoe after betraying his brother. One of the things that makes this movie so great is that it takes place both before and after the first film. Vito Corleone is old and retired and played by Marlon Brando in half of the movie, and in his young man form, he is portrayed by Robert DeNiro. After meeting the very powerful Vito in the first *Godfather* movie, it is great to see his violent, early 1920s rise to power. This drink, like an offer from the don, is something you can't refuse.

RUSHMORE

Whiskey Soda

1 ½ ounces whiskey
3 ounces soda water

Fill a glass of 6 ounces
or more with ice. Add the
whiskey and the soda water.
Stir lightly with a straw.

Rushmore is Wes Anderson's second big movie after *Bottle Rocket* and the one that made his offbeat, monotone style of humor famous. Max Fischer (Jason Schwartzman in his first role) is both the worst and best student at Rushmore Academy. He is talented, crazy, and tries way too hard to be an adult at fifteen years old. Max also thinks he is in love with the school's new teacher, Rosemary (Olivia Williams). Like in most of his movies, Anderson used a lot of his regular players: Schwartzman, Bill Murray, at least one of the Wilson brothers, to name a few. Owen Wilson helped write the movie, and his brother Luke played Dr. Peter Flynn.

In this particular scene, when some of the characters are eating together, Rosemary asks if the Whiskey Soda ordered to the table was for Max. Max replies, "What's wrong with that? I can write a hit play. Why can't have a little drink to unwind myself?"

Cosmopolitan

2 ounces citrus vodka
½ ounce Cointreau
½ ounce lime juice
1 ounce cranberry juice

In a shaker, add all ingredients and ice. Shake and strain into a chilled martini glass and garnish with a lime slice.

The Cosmopolitan is the signature drink of the show's main character, Carrie Bradshaw (Sarah Jessica Parker). Carrie, Samantha, Charlotte, and Miranda drank a lot of different cocktails during the series' six-year run, but the Cosmo is definitely their favorite. This show aired from 1998 to 2004 and had a total of 94 episodes and two feature-length films. This show had such a huge following that *Sex and the City* is even credited with the Cosmopolitan's current rise in popularity. There is a lot of debate over the origin of this cocktail. Nobody knows for sure, but one commonly held belief is that the Cosmopolitan was invented by a bartender in South Beach, Florida, in the mid-80s. Use Carrie's advice: When life gives you lemons, make a lemon Cosmo!

THE SHINING

Hair of the Dog

Hair of the dog is a term for any alcoholic drink you take the morning after a night of heavy drinking to ease your hangover symptoms. It can be anything alcoholic—usually a bit of whatever gave you the hangover to begin with. The term came from a very old belief that if a sick dog bit you, you had to put some of that same dog's hair in your wound to prevent sickness, or possession, or whatever else ancient people believed was affecting the dog that bit you. So naturally, if you became drunk and now are sick from it, it takes a little of what made you sick to cure what ails you. In *The Shining*, Lloyd, the bartender, gave Jack bourbon on the rocks, which is self-explanatory but remember, when you are drinking alcohol on the rocks, it is important to get a very nice brand. Use as big a piece of ice as you can fit in the glass. It will make the bourbon cold without getting too much water in it. Also, use a short, wide, clear glass. These things really make a big difference.

Jack Nicholson plays Jack Torrance in Stanley Kubrick's 1980 masterpiece of modern horror *The Shining*. Jack is a recovering alcoholic and a writer with a very serious case of writer's block. Jack and his family are the new caretakers of the Overlook Hotel. It is a beautiful place with a very dark past. Jack knew about what happened in the hotel, but he agreed to move in with his family for the winter anyway. Jack soon begins to go crazy. He begins to see and interact with a host of spirits. One spirit in particular helps Jack slip into insanity: Lloyd, "the best goddamned bartender from Timbuktu to Portland, Maine. Or Portland, Oregon, for that matter." Jack eventually goes completely insane and tries to murder his family with an axe. Before all of that, there are a few scenes where Jack is drinking at Lloyd's bar. On one such occasion, Lloyd asks Jack what he would like to drink. Jack says, "The hair of the dog that bit me." When Lloyd asks him if bourbon on the rocks will do, Jack responds, "That'll do it." Bourbon on the rocks isn't a cocktail, I know, but it is a big part of such a great movie. This book would not be complete without it.

GROUNDHOG DAY

Sweet Vermouth on the rocks with a twist

This one is self-explanatory.

Two ounces sweet vermouth in a rocks glass over ice cubes. Because you are drinking just vermouth, be sure to get a very nice, Italian red vermouth. Take a long slice of lemon peel and squeeze it with the peel facing the top of the drink. Squeeze the lemon oil into the drink, rub the peel on the rim of the glass, and drop it in.

Imagine waking up every day to repeat the day before. Again and again. For years. Waking up every day at 6:00 a.m. to the same song (Sonny and Cher's "I've Got You, Babe"). Having the same interactions with the same people over and over again for years. Every day not knowing if the cycle will ever end. It is enough to make anyone crazy. Also, it gives you a lot of chances to impress a girl. In the beginning of the movie, Phil (Bill Murray) originally drinks bourbon on the rocks. Later, after finding out that the favorite drink of Rita (Andie MacDowell) was sweet vermouth on the rocks with a lemon peel twist, he begins to drink that. It is obvious he doesn't like this drink, but he drinks it every day (the same day) for the equivalent of about 10 years' worth of repeating. That's 3,649 times he drank something he didn't like to impress someone. How romantic! From a drinker's point of view, anyway.

Some New Classics

The recipes in this section were created especially for this book to pay tribute to some of pop culture's most iconic characters. These are new drinks created by me as an homage to some of my favorite things in pop culture. They were made with a lot of care, thought, and attention to details to be fairly easy to re-create and to be enjoyed with friends. I hope you like the recipes, and I hope you have a lot of fun putting these drinks together. Remember, preference in flavors of anything is a personal thing. I made these drinks to my tastes, but if you want a drink to be sweeter, add more of the sweet ingredient. If you want it stronger, add more alcohol. The point of any drink is to enjoy drinking it, so feel free to get creative. The important part is to have fun with it.

AMERICAN BEAUTY

G-13

2 ounces white tequila
½ ounce triple sec
¼ ounce simple syrup
½ ounce lemon juice
Splash of crème de violet
A barspoon of fernet
Dash of rose water

Put all ingredients in a shaker with ice. Shake and strain into a chilled martini glass.

Lester Burnham (Kevin Spacey) hates his job. His wife is cheating on him, and his daughter hardly speaks to him. He is stuck, bored, and needs a change. After overhearing his daughter's best friend, a teenage girl whom he is obsessed with, Angela (Mena Suvari), say he would be more attractive if he worked out, Lester begins to lift weights in the garage.

Lester also starts to smoke marijuana that he buys from his daughter's boyfriend from across the street, Ricky Fitts (Wes Bently). Lester's favorite kind of weed that he buys from Ricky is called G-13. The drink is a dark green color with an "herbal" after taste. Also rosewater because the roses are a reoccurring theme in Lester's fantasies about Angela. So, as Ricky once asked Lester, "Do you party?"

BIG TROUBLE IN LITTLE CHINA

Miao Yin

1 ounce orange vodka
¾ ounce peach schnapps
¾ ounce green crème de menthe
Splash of cream

Combine all ingredients in a shaker, shake, and strain into a chilled martini glass.

There were a lot of strange things happening in San Francico's Chinatown during the 1980s—from gambling to prostitution, drugs, and more. According to director John Carpenter, there were also bloody gang fights, sorcerers, monsters, magic, and all other forms of ancient "Chinese black magic." In this crazy fun movie, we meet an ancient evil sorcerer named Lo Pan. Lo Pan had a curse put on him hundreds of years ago, and in order to break the curse, he needs to marry a Chinese girl "with eyes of creamy jade." The same creamy green color as this drink. He finds one, and her name is Miao Yin. Unfortunately for Lo Pan, Miao Yin is already engaged to Wang Chi. Wang Chi (Dennis Dun) just so happens to be old friends with Jack Burton (Kurt Russell), and we all know what happened to anyone going up against Kurt Russell in the 80s. It doesn't end well for Lo Pan. This is one of THE classic 80s action movies. It's full of magic, monsters, action, romance, and a whole lot of Kurt Russell. *Big Trouble in Little China* is definitely a must watch for any fan of campy cult classics.

BATMAN

The Alfred

1 ½ ounces gin
1 ½ ounces Pimms No.1
½ ounce maraschino liqueur
A few drops of fernet

In a mixing glass, add the gin, maraschino, Pimms, and ice. Put the few drops of fernet into an empty glass, coat the inside of the glass, and dump out any excess. Place one big ice cube in the glass and strain the stirred cocktail into the fernet-rinsed glass with the ice cube in it. Garnish with lemon peel.

This drink is homage to Bruce Wayne's ever-faithful butler, Alfred Pennyworth. Alfred's relationship to Wayne has changed with different versions of his origin story. The most widely accepted version is that Alfred is a retired British intelligence agent and was the Wayne family butler before Thomas and Martha (Bruce's patents) were murdered. He then took over as guardian of Bruce and taught him how to be a detective. Here is a strange coincidence. Tony Stark as Iron Man can be seen as Marvel's version of Bruce Wayne, twenty-five years or so after Batman was introduced in *Detective Comics* #27. He was also a billionaire orphan and had no powers, except for fighting, wealth, intelligence, and an amazing suit of his own invention. In the *Iron Man* story, Stark has a butler named Jarvis. Alfred's father, who talked him into coming out of retirement, was a long-time professional butler also named Jarvis.

Anyway, back to drinking. For this drink, I added some very British ingredients—the gin and Pimms—for a very British character. The only alcohol I can remember Alfred drinking is fernet in the last of *The Dark Knight* trilogy (2012). This drink is strong, classy, and understated. Just like the Wayne family's quietly awesome butler.

THE AVENGERS

Pearl Barley

1 ounce blended scotch
½ ounce cream
3 ½ ounces hot tea

Combine all ingredients in a
teacup of at least 6 ounces.
Stir "anticlockwise."

One of the best, campiest, most
entertaining espionage/sci-fi
shows ever made, *The Avengers*
began in 1960. Originally in this
series' first season, the impossibly
smooth, bowler hat–wearing super
spy John Steed (Patrick Macnee)
was the assistant to Dr. David Keel.
From the second season on, Steed
was in charge, with a few changing
female assistants. Most notable
was the smart, sexy, and fierce
Emma Peel (Diana Rigg). In the
episode "Dial a Deadly Number,"
Emma Peel is trying to make tea at Steed's
home. She needs help because all of the jars in
Steed's kitchen are mislabeled. He keeps his tea
in a jar labeled "pearl barley." In one episode,
when Mrs. Peel asks Steed if he would like a
drink, he replies, "Intravenously!" Also, Tara
King replaces Peel as Steed's companion in the
beginning of the sixth season. On the way out,
Peel tells King that Steed prefers his tea stirred
"anticlockwise." In the 1998 *The Avengers* movie,
Uma Thurman plays Emma Peel, and Ralph
Fiennes is Steed. In one scene, Steed has a tea
dispenser in his Bentley. The tea comes out with
milk already added, so I assume that is how he
prefers to drink it.

JAWS

Captain Quint's Grog

2 ounces gold rum
½ ounce simple syrup
Half a lime
Soda water
Barspoon of grenadine

In a short, wide whiskey glass, add the simple syrup, the half lime cut into four pieces, and a splash of soda water. Muddle until the limes are juiced. Add the rum, fill with ice, stir gently, top off with more soda water, and drop in the grenadine.

"We're gonna need a bigger boat." *Jaws* was one of those movies that did not lose its effect over time. Watching *Jaws* today is still just as intense as it was in the movie theaters in 1975. The great characters, the lines, and of course the shark. We hardly see the shark, and that somehow makes it a lot more terrifying. One of the best characters is Captain Quint with his ship *Orca*. He is a retired Navy veteran, and he was on board the USS *Indianapolis* when it was sunk by the Japanese in 1945. Grog was a traditional drink for the navy after it was invented by Admiral Vernon in the early 1700s. Originally it was 4 parts water to 1 part dark rum with lime juice and sugar to taste. In the book, after Quint harpoons the beast, it dives into the ocean. Quint's leg is tangled in the line, and so he goes down with it and drowns. In the movie, however, when the shark jumps onto the boat, it bites Quint in half. It is a very bloody scene, and this is why his grog has turned red. So, in the words of ol' Quint himself, "Here's to swimmin' with bow-legged women!"

DOCTOR WHO

Rekkar

1 ounce gin
½ ounce tonic water
1 glass of a light beer

Pour your gin into a shot glass. Add the tonic water last. Cover the glass with your hand and hit the bottom of it on the table. Shout "HEY!" and take the shot. Follow the shot with a drink of your beer.

In the Doctor Who book The Shakedown, Bernice Summerfield is studying abroad on the planet Centauri. The inhabitants of Centauri are like giant bugs with human characteristics. The workers in the city are like giant beetles, slightly smaller than a person. During a night of drinking in one of the worker beetles' bars with Professor Lazlo Zemar, the professor describes something called "rekkar" as "a basic form of booze available in most cultures on most planets. A distilled white spirit, colorless and tasteless, with a kick like Soggorian swamp-elephant!" He then tells her that the ritual for drinking this is to pour some rekkar into a short thick glass, hit it on the table so it gets fizzy, and shout the word "HEY!" right before you drink the whole shot. You chase the shot with a drink of beer to "stop from burning out the back of your throat." Rekkar is said to be very strong for humans, but the native Centaurians can drink it straight with no beer chaser or apparent reactions—until they all start fighting each other, and Bernice and the professor have to leave the bar in a hurry! Don't forget the part about yelling "HEY!" before you drink. We do not want to offend any giant drunken beetles.

EVIL DEAD

Boomstick

1 ½ ounces bourbon
¼ ounce simple syrup
¾ ounce Cointreau
3 ounces boiling water
Tiny pinch of cinnamon powder
Absinthe rinse
Orange peel

Boil water. When it's boiling, fill up a glass of 6 ounces or more that has a handle. Let it sit for a minute to heat the glass. Dump the water, pour a little absinthe in the now hot glass, and swirl it around until the glass is coated inside. Dump out any excess. Add simple syrup, cinnamon, Cointreau, and bourbon. Stir lightly until everything is mixed together. Add the boiling water last. Stir lightly and garnish with a cinnamon stick and an orange peel, first spraying the oil from the peel on the top of the drink.

All three movies in the Evil Dead trilogy are great. The first two are basically the same. In a cabin in the woods listening to a recording of someone reading from the *Necronomicon*, everything except for our hero Ash (Bruce Campbell) becomes not only dead, but evil as well. In the third movie, *Army of Darkness,* a time portal sends Ash into a medieval alternate reality. Lord Arthur is about to be attacked by an evil army of "deadites." Luckily, Ash traveled through time with his car, his chainsaw hand, and his shotgun, which he calls his "boomstick." At one point in *Army of Darkness*, Ash is being attacked by a group of very small evil versions of himself. They stab him, shoot him, and burn his face. (Well, actually they trip Ash, and he falls on the stove. He has to use a spatula to get his own face off of the griddle.) After he is tied to the floor, one of the tiny Ashes dives into his mouth and starts to fight him from in his stomach. To fight this tiny, evil clone, Ash drinks a kettle of boiling water! Genius! Also, for the drink I wanted a cinnamon "boomstick" and the simple syrup because, well, "Gimme some sugar, baby." Also, the Cointreau and the absinthe rinse are a nod to another great drink for any cocktail geek that might get the reference. "Alright. Who wants some?"

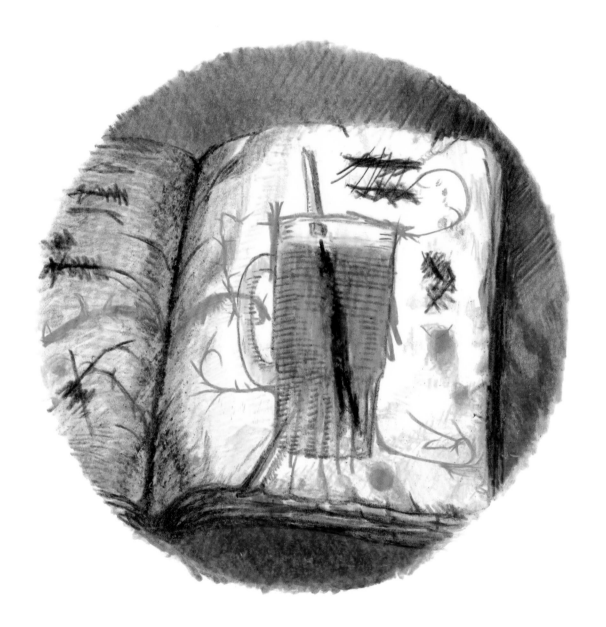

ADDAMS FAMILY

Morticia

2 ½ ounces Hendrick's gin
1 ½ ounces St. Germain
elderflower liqueur
1 barspoon absinthe
Dash of rose water
Splash of soda water

Pour everything except for the
soda water into a mixing glass.
Stir and strain into a coupe glass
and splash soda water on top.

They're creepy, they're kooky, mysterious, and spooky. They are *The Addams Family*. They are a very close, loving family of macabre characters created by Charles Addams and who appeared first as a series of comics in the *New Yorker* magazine in 1938. The immediate family consisted of Gomez, Morticia, and their two kids, Pugsly and Wednesday ("who is full of woe," according to Edward Gorey). There is also the tall monstrous butler Lurch, Grandmama, a living hand with no body attached named Thing, and Morticia's uncle Fester, who in the movie was made to be Gomez's older brother. With kids who are always (lovingly) trying to kill each other and a carnivorous plant (an African strangler, to be exact) named Cleopatra who needs regular feedings, Morticia might need a drink to wind down. So here is a drink for the matriarch of this crazy family. Something elegant, slightly medicinal, and will make use of all those roses Morticia has cut from their stems. I'll leave you with what Morticia insists are "more than just pretty words"—the Addams family credo: *Sic gorgiamus allos subjectatos nunc,* which is almost Latin for "We gladly feast on those who would subdue us."

NIGHTMARE ON ELM STREET

Krueger Bomb

1 ounce bourbon
½ ounce cinnamon schnapps
A float of overproof rum
(such as Bacardi 151)
4 ounces Red Bull energy drink

Pour the Red Bull into an
empty pint glass. Pour the
bourbon and cinnamon
schnapps into a shot glass and
float the overproof rum on
top. Very carefully light the
shot on fire. Let it sit burning for a second
or two for effect, gently blow the flame
out, and drop the shot into the glass of
Red Bull. Cheer your friends and drink the
whole thing. Please be careful that the shot
glass doesn't come sliding forward and hit
your teeth.

Nightmare on Elm Street is one
of the most classic horror movie
series. The evil, burned, and dead
murderer-turned-demon, Freddy
Krueger (the legendary Robert
Englund) is back from the dead
and killing teenagers in their
dreams. The victims in this series
can't die unless they fall asleep,
so they are all constantly looking
for ways to stay awake. Red Bull
should do the trick. Fire is a
recurring theme in this series. It is
how Freddy died in the beginning,
so it seems necessary for this
drink to have some fire as well. Also, putting
the word "bomb" in a drink's name usually
means that it is a shot of something dropped
into a glass of something else. The Nightmare
on Elm Street series is remembered for having
some of the most outrageous one-line jokes
and a lot of very memorable on-screen deaths.
On one occasion, Krueger turned a girl into
a cockroach and smashed her in a giant bug
trap. In another, he used his claws to scratch a
chalkboard so loudly that it made a kid's head
explode! Freddy Krueger continues to haunt the
dreams of movie fans, but it's OK. Remember,
he can't get you if you don't fall asleep!

STAR WARS: REVENGE OF THE SITH

Sith Banter

1 ounce crème de noyaux
2 ounces raspberry vodka
1 barspoon grenadine
¼ ounce lemon juice
Splash of soda water

Combine all ingredients except for the soda water in a shaker with ice. Shake and strain into a short, wide glass with one big ice cube.

The Sith are the followers of the dark side of the force—the bad guys, in other words. They are out to rule the galaxy and exterminate every last Jedi. Their power is only matched by their hatred of the Jedi. The Sith were first dark Jedi who were banished to a far-off planet called Korriban. Once there, they enslaved a race of red-skinned natives called "Sith." Later, these dark Jedi changed the name of their independent dark philosophy to match their now loyal subjects. Many years later, legendary Sith master Darth Bane, in order to concentrate dark force power, created the rule of two: Only two Sith may exist at any time—a master and an apprentice, i.e., Darth Sidious (Emperor Palpatine) and Darth Vader. The Sith almost always use a red light sabre and wear black cloaks. Red seems to be a recurring theme with the Sith, so naturally their cocktail would have to be not only strong, but bright red as well.

STAR WARS: RETURN OF THE JEDI

Revenge of the Jedi

2 ounces white rum
1 ¼ ounces melon liqueur
¾ ounce lemon juice
1 barspoon limoncello
A splash of lemon-lime flavored soda

Pour all ingredients except for the lemon-lime soda into a glass of 6 ounces or more. Fill with ice, stir, and last, top off with the lemon-lime soda.

The Jedi are the patient, logical, force-sensitive knights for peace and harmony in the Star Wars galaxy—in other words, the good guys. They study and utilize the light side of the force and are the opposite side of the force spectrum of the Sith. Naturally, the Jedi and the Sith are sworn enemies with very different views on how the power of the force should be utilized. The Jedi knight's traditional weapon of choice is a lightsaber. The various Jedi use a few different colors for their lightsabers but never red. In episode 4 (the first movie released), young Jedi apprentice Luke Skywalker gets a hand-me-down blue lightsaber from Obi-Wan Kenobi. By the end of *Return of the Jedi* (originally *Revenge of the Jedi* but changed right before release), Luke has constructed his own green lightsaber, like master Yoda's, and has completed his training. It would seem that, in drinks or lightsabers, bright green is a popular color choice for a Jedi master.

THE WARRIORS

Initiation

1 ounce bourbon
1 ounce apple schnapps
1 ounce cranberry juice
Dash of angostura bitters
Splash of soda water

Except for the soda water, combine all ingredients in a mixing glass full of ice. Stir and strain into a short, wide glass with one big ice cube. Splash the soda water on top.

This is one of those must-see movies. So many classic characters and great lines, and the fight scenes are awesome. Almost everything about this movie is cool. Every gang is so different and imaginative—from the Moonrunners to the Turnbull AC's and those tough chicks, the Lizzies. Not to mention the maybe most memorable, the Baseball Furies, who look like scary clowns in baseball uniforms. It's 1979, and New York City is filled with all sorts of gangs like this. Cyrus, the leader of the biggest gang, the Riffs, has called a peace meeting with nine delegates from each of the 100 bigger gangs. Cyrus gets shot, and the police ambush the meeting. In all of the chaos, one gang, the Warriors, get wrongfully accused of shooting Cyrus. The Warriors go on the run, and every gang and New York police officer is on the lookout for them. The various gangs all stay updated on the search through a radio DJ, voiced by the unmistakable Lynne Thigpen. The Warriors have to fight their way across New York City to get to their home turf, Coney Island. In this world, it is important to always wear your colors to represent your gang. This drink is not for wimps. It's classic Warriors maroon and tastes like the Big Apple. Can you dig it?

THE HUNGER GAMES

Nightlock Cocktail

2 ounces blueberry vodka
½ ounce lemon juice
½ ounce simple syrup
Dash of orange bitters
Splash of soda water
3 blueberries

Combine vodka, lemon juice, sugar, and bitters in a shaker. Add ice, shake, and strain into a chilled martini glass. Top off with soda water. Drop in the three blueberries.

At the end of the first Hunger Games movie, Katniss (Jennifer Lawrence) and Peeta (Josh Hutcherson) are the last two contenders in the 74th annual Hunger Games. They have beaten twenty-two other tribute contenders from eleven other districts (some better trained than others). As a protest, they both threaten to eat nightlock berries to commit suicide so, for the first time, the Hunger Games would have no winner. When Katniss pulls the berries out of her bag, they look very similar to blueberries. Before they can eat the poisonous nightlock, it is decided that the Hunger Games will have two winners. Also, for making such a mess of the games, President Snow offers Seneca Crane a bowl of nightlock berries, insisting he take his own life. Enjoy!

I LOVE LUCY

Ricky Ricardo

2 ½ ounces dark Cuban rum
1 ¼ ounces sweet vermouth
2 dashes of orange bitters
Orange peel

**Combine all ingredients
in a mixing glass. Add ice,
stir, and strain into a chilled
martini glass. Garnish with
an orange peel.**

Ricky Ricardo (Desi Arnaz) is
the Cuban husband of Lucy
(Lucille Ball). Ricky is trying to
make a name for himself as an
entertainer and musician. They
both live in an apartment in
Manhattan. The show's other
main characters are Lucy and
Ricky's neighbors, Fred and Ethel.
Lucy (and sometimes Ethel)
get various jobs throughout the
show. Whether it's stomping
grapes for wine, working on
the line at a chocolate factory,
or making a commercial
for Vitameatavegamin, it almost always
ends in Lucy messing everything up, and
sometimes she cries about it very loudly and
exaggeratedly. With all the trouble Lucy gets
into, I thought Ricky could use a drink while
he listens to Lucy's "serious explanation." This
drink is like another very famous New York
drink but with a Cuban twist. Also, the orange
bitters and orange peel garnish because we
can't forget about Lucy.

DIRTY HARRY

The Signal

1 ½ ounces Irish cream liqueur
½ ounce coffee liqueur
4 ounces hot black coffee

Pour all ingredients into a coffee mug of 6 ounces or more. Serve hot.

San Francisco detective "Dirty" Harry Callahan is a tough as nails, super masculine, plays by his own rules, shoot-first-and-ask-questions-later kind of guy. Harry always drinks his coffee black, but in *Sudden Impact*, when his favorite waitress, Loretta, fills his coffee with sugar, it is a signal that there is trouble at the Acorn Café, so this coffee drink is supposed to be sweet.

Anyway, Harry leaves and tastes the coffee outside. He gets the hint, sneaks into the café through the back door, and some unlucky punks then get to meet Callahan's iconic .44 magnum Smith & Wesson. It is one of the most memorable scenes in the series. *Sudden Impact* is the fourth in the Dirty Harry series and the only one to be directed by Harry himself, Clint Eastwood. This is the kind of coffee that will "make your day," but just don't react the same way Harry did when he tasted the coffee. He spit it out.

IRON MAN

Tony Stark

2 ½ ounces single malt Scotch
¾ ounce Lillet Blanc
¾ ounce red port wine
Dash of angostura bitters

Combine all ingredients in a mixing glass. Add ice, stir, and strain into a short, wide whiskey glass with one big ice cube.

"Give me a Scotch. I'm starving!" Tony Stark was a heavy drinker in the beginning of the Iron Man story, and when he drank, he preferred to drink Scotch. Knowing Tony Stark, it was most likely very expensive and rare Scotch. Tony is the "genius billionaire playboy philanthropist" behind "The Invincible Iron Man." His first appearance was in *Tales of Suspense* #39 in March 1963, but in 1968 Iron Man got his own comic book series, and he is still, to this day, one of Marvel's most popular characters. Stark was one of the founding members of Marvel's Avengers, but after calling for super-humans to register, he starts a civil war with Captain America. If Tony Stark had a drink named after him, it would be fancy, expensive, strong, and made with Scotch. Tony wouldn't be able to drink it now, because he quit drinking in the episode titled "Demon in a Bottle," but maybe his butler, Mr. Jarvis, should have a few. He's earned it.

MAD MAX

Auntie's Pear Juice

¼ ounce lemon juice
1 packet raw crystalized sugar
(the kind you find in little
packets at coffee shops—the
packet with the brown, bigger
crystals of sugar)
2 ounces pear vodka
A splash of soda water

In a shaker, add the vodka, the simple
syrup, and the lime juice. Shake and strain
into a chilled martini glass. Splash soda
on top and sprinkle the sugar in last, so it
doesn't mix in and stays at the bottom of
the drink.

In the third (and arguably the best) film in the Mad Max series, the road warrior finds himself in Bartertown. This post-apocalyptic trading colony is run by a woman named Auntie (Tina Turner). Right after meeting Auntie, Max is offered a bowl of pears and some water. Fruit is very hard to come by in this vision of the future; offering a bowl of it to a guest is a big show of power. Auntie bites into a pear as a signal for her guards to attack Max. This is a test to see if the "raggedy man" is up to the challenge of taking out Auntie's only rival for control in Bartertown, Master Blaster, in the Thunderdome. This drink is pear flavored and has a splash of water (also rare in Bartertown). Almost everything in this future is dirty or has a layer of sand or dust on it. The sugar in the bottom of the drink gives the effect of sand that might have gotten into Auntie's glass as it is everywhere else in Bartertown. Now, ladies and gentlemen, boys and girls . . . DRINKIN' TIME IS HERE!

WIZARD OF OZ

Emerald Palace

¾ ounce melon liqueur
¾ ounce Goldschläger
4 ounces or so of sparkling wine
(champagne if you've got it)

Pour the melon liqueur and the
Goldschläger in a champagne
flute of 6 ounces or more.
Top with sparkling wine.

In this classic story, a young girl from Kansas, Dorothy, "and her little dog too!" are transported via tornado to the magical Land of Oz. It is a land filled with various imaginative characters. Dorothy makes friends with some of the different residents. Most important, the cowardly lion, the heart-less tin man, and the scarecrow without a brain. After some advice from the good witch Glenda, these friends embark on a journey down the yellow brick road to the Emerald Palace, where the wizard of Oz lives. This drink is light and fun like the movie, and in the end, it's green like the Emerald Palace, with pieces of the yellow brick road floating around. Also the good witch Glenda travels around in a floating bubble, much like the bubbles in this drink. It is a drink fit for the great and powerful Oz! Just pay no attention to that man behind the curtain.

A CLOCKWORK ORANGE

Moloko Plus

1 ½ ounces orange vodka
1 barspoon sugar
½ ounce egg white
¼ ounce orange juice
¼ ounce lemon juice
1 ounce cream
Dash of orange flower water
Orange peel

Dry shake the cream, sugar, and egg whites vigorously for 10 to 15 seconds. Add the rest of the ingredients and ice, and shake vigorously again, and strain into a Collins glass with ice. Garnish with an orange peel.

A Clockwork Orange is one of those rare stories that makes you feel sympathetic for a very bad person. The novel by Anthony Burgess was mind-blowing when it came out in 1962, but Stanley Kubrick made a more memorable, very controversial, and visually unforgettable film version in 1971. The main character and our narrator, Alex, was played by Malcolm McDowell. Before a night out, Alex and his droogs always stop in the Korova Milk Bar for a few glasses of moloko plus. In the story, the milk will "sharpen you up and make you ready for a bit of the old ultra-violence." At the Korova Milk Bar, you can get a variety of milks with various chemicals mixed in. Alex and his gang are mixing "moloko vellocet," milk with some kind of opiate. For our purposes, we use gin.

In Anthony Burgess's hellish vision of a future where violent gangs control the night, we follow one of the most dangerous and sadistic sixteen-year-olds in literature. The signature all-white outfit, with black bowler hat, codpiece, and fake eyelashes on one eye, is a look that will forever be instantly recognizable.

OSS 117: LOST IN RIO

Caïpirinha 117

2 ounces cachaça
½ ounce Cointreau
½ of a lime cut into five
or six pieces
Thin orange slice
2 sugar cubes
Splash of soda water

In the bottom of a short, wide
glass, drop in the limes, the
orange slice, and the sugar.
Muddle them all together and add ice. Add
cachaça, Cointreau, and soda water and stir.
Serve in the same glass you made it in.

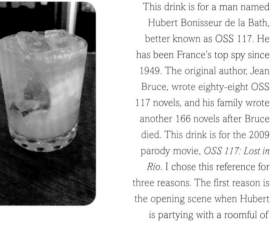

This drink is for a man named Hubert Bonisseur de la Bath, better known as OSS 117. He has been France's top spy since 1949. The original author, Jean Bruce, wrote eighty-eight OSS 117 novels, and his family wrote another 166 novels after Bruce died. This drink is for the 2009 parody movie, *OSS 117: Lost in Rio*. I chose this reference for three reasons. The first reason is the opening scene when Hubert is partying with a roomful of only young Chinese women and him, drinking and dancing until some Chinese gunmen come in and stop the party. The second reason is CIA agent Bill Tremendous. If you have seen the movie, you will know exactly what I am talking about. The last reason is because cachaça is really delicious with lime and orange. The Caïparinha is Brazil's national drink. This one has a definitely French twist. The OSS novels were serious spy/action-adventure novels. The first even pre-dated Ian Fleming's first 007 novel. The two movies starring Jean Dujardin are funny parodies of the novels, but they were also many people's first introduction to the world of OSS 117. Me included.

PEE-WEE'S BIG ADVENTURE

1 ½ ounces white tequila
½ ounce lime juice
½ ounce simple syrup
¾ ounce egg white
¾ ounce cream
½ ounce grenadine

Put the egg white, the cream, and the sugar into a shaker and give it a dry shake for 10 to 15 seconds. Next, add the rest of the ingredients and some ice. Shake again very hard for another 15 seconds or so, and pour into a chilled martini glass, and garnish with a cherry.

Paul Reubens and Phil Hartman came up with the Pee-wee Herman character, but it was Reubens that gave him life. Pee-wee was one of those rare characters that entertained both adults and kids alike. His crazy, amazing, brilliant TV show *Pee-wee's Playhouse* was intended for a younger audience, but some of the biggest stars of the time had a part in making the show. Cyndi Lauper sang the title song, Laurence Fishburne and Phil Hartman were recurring characters, and every episode had a different soundtrack by a different artist. Devo's Mark Mothersbaugh even did one episode. Apart from the show, Pee-wee also starred in a few movies. Tim Burton directed the classic *Pee-wee's Big Adventure*. In that movie, someone has stolen Pee-wee's most valued possession: his bike! When he realizes that his bike has been taken out of town, he goes on a road trip to get it back. This drink is named after Pee-wee's bike, the X-1. Also, it is very hard to guess Pee-wee's age. He lives in a house alone, but he acts like a child, so this drink is sweet like a kid's drink but strong like an adult's drink. Also, it's red like the color of the bike—well, it's a lighter color; closer to pink actually—but you get it. In one scene, Pee-wee has gotten into some trouble with a gang of bikers at a bar. They ask him if has any last requests, and he does. He gets some white platform shoes and does a very . . . memorable dance on the bar to the 1958 song "Tequila" by the Champs. Also, Pee-wee's big adventure begins in San Francisco. It isn't mentioned, but when Pee-wee looks at a map of his town, it is a map of San Francisco that he is looking at.

DIE HARD

Nakatomi Punch

First, make syrup with:
200 grams of sugar
200 grams of water
1 Fuji apple, chopped
½ fennel bulb, also chopped
Lemon peel

While you're preparing this punch, you should be heating the punch bowl. Also, an easy-to-follow rule for ingredient ratios when making a good punch is this: one of sour, two of sweet. Three of strong and four of weak. With that in mind, in another container, mix:
6 ounces fresh lemon juice
12 ounces of your newly made syrup
2 ¼ cups Japanese whiskey

Mix them all together and pour them into your heated punch bowl. Next, add 3 cups of boiling water and gently mix everything. Top off with some slices of apple and slices of lemon peel for garnish. Serves six to eight people. Grate some of a cinnamon stick into each full cup and put the rest of the stick in the cup. All of the amounts for the ingredients are approximate. In the end, make it to your taste. Add more water, or sugar, or juice or use less. As long as it tastes good.

It's Christmas Eve, 1988. Time for the Nakatomi Corporation's holiday party! All is going fine. Everyone is drinking, doing drugs, or hooking up in their offices. That is until Hans Gruber (Alan Rickman) and his heavily armed gang of bad guys crash the party. Too bad for Hans, one of the employees is married to NYPD officer, John McClane (Bruce Willis). McClane may not have any shoes, but he is clever enough to take out all the bad guys one at a time. *Die Hard* is still considered one of the most loved holiday movies in the United States and also one of the best action movies series ever. Before all of the action, the employees at the Nakatomi holiday party are all drinking some kind of punch, so in honor of what looked like a pretty fun party, I made a Nakatomi punch. Remember, this recipe is for serving six to eight people. Punch bowls are meant to be shared with friends. "Welcome to the party, pal!"

PLANET OF THE APES

Dr. Zaius

2 ounces aged rum
1 ounce crème de banana
1 ounce lime juice

Put all ingredients into a shaker with ice. Shake and strain into a short wide clear glass with one big ice cube.

The story of a planet where apes have evolved from the humans, and humans live like animals in the jungle was first written by French author Pierre Boulle in 1963. The first film version was done in 1968 and starred Charlton Heston. Dr. Zaius is the main antagonist in this series. He is sort of an evolved version of an orangutan. He has reddish-blonde fur and a brown leather outfit. Dr. Zaius was one of the few who knew the real past of the planet, and how the humans were the dominant species, and how they were the masters of the apes. He knew how the humans destroyed most of the planet, along with most of themselves, leaving the Earth for the apes to take over. He also thought that, if given the chance, the humans would put the apes back in chains and ruin the world again. He wasn't a bad ape. He was just trying to protect his people and their way of life. It was just his methods that were a little extreme. He thought that the only way for the apes to continue to thrive was to eliminate all the remaining humans. He thought they were a nuisance, an inferior species, and a harm to the planet and the ape's civilization. This drink is for Dr. Zaius, because, well, he might be right. It's a take on an old recipe called "The Doctor" but made more for ape taste.

PSYCHO

Mother Bates

3 ounces dry gin
1 ounce elderflower liqueur
1 teaspoon crème de violette

Stir with ice and strain into a
chilled martini glass.

Psycho is Alfred Hitchcock's terribly deranged masterpiece about a man with an affection for taxidermy who really, really loves his mother. Norman Bates (Anthony Perkins) runs the Bates Motel. His mother, the widow Norma Bates, presumably owns the hotel, although we only hear her screaming at Norman. We don't see her until the end of the film.

She is the inspiration for Norman's obsession. She is always calling him from the house up on the hill behind the hotel. She is seemingly equally obsessed with her son, trying to protect him from everything. When Norman starts to have feelings for a motel guest Marion Crane, Mother doesn't take it so well, and Crane gets killed in the shower in one of the most memorable murder scenes in movie history. For a drink in homage to the elderly, the insane, the deceased Mrs. Bates, I wanted to make something, well, floral and dry.

WHO FRAMED ROGER RABBIT?

Roger Rabbit

2 ounces vodka
4 ounces carrot juice
½ ounce jalapeño syrup
Pinch of salt
Pinch of black pepper
A dash of angostura bitters
Syrup

For making the jalapeño syrup,
in a saucepan, mix:
100 grams of white sugar
100 grams of water

After the sugar is all dissolved, add one-half jalapeño, chopped, and juice of half a lime. Simmer all together on low heat for 10 minutes or so. Strain the liquid into a ready container.

In a glass of 8 ounces or more, add the syrup, the salt, the pepper, the bitters, and the vodka. Stir and then add ice and carrot juice. Garnish with celery, and whatever else sounds good, and that you have already in your kitchen.

Who Framed Roger Rabbit? is a movie full of alcohol. The main character, Eddie Valiant (Bob Hoskins), is an alcoholic. This is a 1947 Hollywood where humans and cartoons live and work together. Roger Rabbit and Eddie are on the run, trying to prove Roger's innocence in the murder of Marvin Acme. Eddie prefers Scotch on the rocks (and he means ice!). Roger, however, can't handle his Scotch. In one scene, Eddie tricks him into drinking a glass of Scotch in order to escape from Judge Doom (Christopher Lloyd) and his weasel henchmen. Roger changes color, turns into a steam whistle, blows up, and various other things you might expect a cartoon character to do in reaction to having a shot of Scotch. It seems Roger Rabbit needs something a little softer on the palate. Something a rabbit would probably like. One other thing: The best time for having this drink is definitely during the day. It is a recipe meant for afternoon drinking, and it really isn't something you'd want to drink at night. FYI.

BACK TO THE FUTURE

Marty McFly

2 ounces bourbon
5 or more ounces Pepsi
Dash angostura bitters

Fill a glass of 10 ounces or
more with ice. Add bourbon
and fill to the top with Pepsi.
Dash angostura bitters on top.

Back to the Future is one of those series that everyone needs to see. (Yes, even the third one.) In the second movie, Doc (Christopher Lloyd) and Marty McFly (Michael J. Fox) travel to October 21, 2015—a future full of flying cars, hover boards, and automatic drying clothes. Marty follows his unknowing future son to Café 80s. When his waiter (Michael Jackson on a floating TV) asks him what he would like, Marty specifically orders Pepsi. Also, in the first movie in the series, before going into the school dance, Marty is in his car with his mom/date, Lorraine (Lea Thompson). They are both taking sips from a bottle of whiskey before Biff (Thomas F. Wilson) interrupts the pre-dance tippling and gets knocked out by Marty's future father. It's a long story. Anyhow, with all of this, it seems pretty obvious what Marty McFly would drink if he had the choice. The angostura bitters in the drink is just because it tastes good, and we all like drinks that taste good.

THE ROCKY HORROR PICTURE SHOW

Sweet Transvestite

Fill a champagne flute three quarters of the way with champagne. Put a few drops of Campari on a sugar cube and drop it in to the champagne. Add one barspoon of grenadine.

The Rocky Horror Picture Show is THE cult classic. The movie and the play both are reenacted on stage almost every year in almost every American city. When you see the play live, the audience has its own script. They bring props and dress in costumes too, interacting with the cast as the play goes on. The story is set in an old mansion where a big party is going on. Tim Curry plays the owner of the mansion and host of the party, Frank-N-Furter. The "sweet transvestite from transsexual Transylvania" is also a mad scientist. He has created a muscular man to marry him and be his personal plaything. The party is to celebrate the birth of Frank-N-Furter's creature "Rocky." Everyone at the party is drinking some champagne and having a good time doing a dance called the Time Warp. That's when some unexpected guests show up, and things get weird. This movie has everything: aliens, murders, dancing, sex (of all kinds), and some very unforgettable musical numbers. Whenever we see Frank-N-Furter drinking, he is drinking red-colored champagne, so that is what I have made. This is a very tasty drink. You'll have a taste, and you'll want more! (More, more, more!)

THE SIMPSONS

Marge Simpson

1 ounce orange juice
2 ounces peach vodka
½ ounce triple sec
½ ounce sweet and sour
1 barspoon blue curaçao

In a tall, thin, cylindrical clear glass of 6 ounces, pour in the sweet and sour and the orange juice. In a separate glass, mix the vodka, the triple sec, and the curaçao. In the glass with the orange juice, fill with ice. Slowly pour the vodka mixture on top so it floats and makes an obvious yellow bottom and a blue top.

Marge Simpson is TV's most patient and loving mother. To be the ever-faithful wife of a guy like Homer Simpson and the mother of a kid like Bart takes a very special lady. Marge's two daughters, Lisa and Maggie, are more like their mother: smart, sweet, and slightly obsessive.

With her signature tall blue hair and raspy voice, Marge is the glue holding the Simpson family together. She puts up with a lot. For almost thirty years she has been raising three very rambunctious children who never grow up! If anyone deserves her own drink, it's Marge Simpson. This drink—if you've made it right— looks like Marge Simpson, with her tall blue hair and her yellow face. Also, when you stir it up, it turns the green of her dress.

GHOSTBUSTERS

Toasted Stay Puft

½ ounce pineapple juice
1 ½ ounces vanilla vodka
1 barspoon Rose's lime juice
½ ounce simple syrup
½ ounce egg white
¼ ounce cream

Combine all ingredients in a shaker. Shake vigorously for about 15 seconds or until it's frothy. For a garnish, put one big marshmallow (or a few small ones) on a toothpick, and briefly light them on fire, and put them out. Put it in the drink and serve.

Poor Peter Venkman (Bill Murray). The woman he loves, Dana Barrett (Sigourney Weaver) lives in a building designed after World War I by a cult-leading architect to be the gateway for summoning the Sumerian god of destruction, Gozer. She then gets possessed as "The Gatekeeper" and falls for a nerd with glowing eyes, calling himself "The Keymaster." There are a lot more ghosts involved, and two dog-like horned beasts making things worse. Good thing he's got help! Egon Spengler (Harold Ramis), Winston Zeddemore (Ernie Hudson), and Raymond Stantz (Dan Aykroyd). When the voice of a demon woman covered in bubbles told the team that the destructor Gozer was going to come in any form they thought of, Stantz thought of something so puffy and delicious that after they "crossed streams" to defeat it, someone came along 30 years later and made a cocktail after it. Thanks, Stantz!

Aldebaran Whiskey

3 ounces white rum
½ ounce simple syrup
½ ounce lime juice
½ ounce melon liqueur

Pour all ingredients into a shaker with ice. Shake and strain into a short, wide glass with one big ice cube.

Alderbaran whiskey is the bright green alcoholic drink that pops up in every Star Trek series at some point. Quark keeps barrels of it on Deep Space Nine, and Guinan loves the stuff. Captain Picard gave a bottle to Scotty as a gift once as well. Data offered Scotty a glass of Alderbaran whiskey and uses the same words to describe it as Scotty did in episode 50 "By Any Other Name," "It's . . . green." In that classic episode, hostile aliens on board the *Enterprise* "have taken a human form and are therefore having human reaction." Scotty has the idea to get the leader of the invading species drunk because it will react like a human to alcohol. After a bottle of Saurian brandy, Scotty moves on to a mysterious bottle full of a strong green alcohol. When he is asked of its contents, Scotty can only describe the liquid's color: green. After the (assumed) Alderbaran whiskey is gone, Scotty moves on to a very dusty bottle of Scotch. At the end of this bottle, the alien passes out drunk while Scotty is still sitting up in his chair. Scotty kisses and thanks his empty Scotch bottle: "We did it, you and me. Put him right under the table."

TEENAGE MUTANT NINJA TURTLES

Cowabunga Cocktail

2 ounces gin
½ ounce lime juice
¾ ounce maraschino liqueur
¼ ounce Midori
5 drops angostura bitters

In a shaker, add ice, gin, lime juice, maraschino, and Midori. Shake and strain into a chilled cocktail glass. Lightly drop the bitters on top. Put just the tip of a straw into the cocktail—maybe 1 centimeter—and lightly stir the bitters, so it remains in a layer on top of the drink. Garnish with a purple grape, a cherry, a blueberry, or an orange slice, depending on your mood.

They are teenage . . . mutant . . . ninja . . . turtles with a giant rat as a master, and they love pizza. It is beautiful. It is amazing. It was an idea that was so absurd that it should have never worked, but it did! Even now, 30 years or so after the first *Ninja Turtles* comic, everyone's favorite "heroes in a half-shell" are being loved by a whole new generation. Kids today are being entertained by the same characters that entertained their parents. They have come in many forms: print, cartoons, live action movies with *Turtle*-costumed actors, and, most recently, computer-animated in a big budget Hollywood action blockbuster. This drink, if done correctly, should be green with a brown layer on top. In a martini glass, it sort of resembles a turtle. Cheers! Or, if you prefer, cowabunga!

Milk of Poppy

2 ½ ounces citrus vodka
¼ ounce orgeat syrup
¼ ounce lemon juice
½ ounce triple sec
3 to 5 mint leaves

In the bottom of a mixing glass, muddle the mint leaves and the lemon juice. Add the rest of the ingredients and ice to the glass. Shake everything and strain it into a chilled martini glass. Garnish with a few fresh mint leaves.

Milk of poppy is the go-to painkiller in George R.R. Martin's medieval fantasy continent of Westeros. It is made by the Maesters, who brew this potion from crushed poppy flowers, and it is said to be milky and white in color. It is a very powerful anesthetic. In a big enough dose, it could render the drinker unconscious enough for surgery.

Milk of poppy is mentioned several times in both the HBO series and the series of novels. Sir Gregor "The Mountain" drinks it for headaches, and Robb Stark made a point to steal the whole supply of it from a castle known as The Crag. Sansa Stark even tried to use the effects of milk of poppy as an excuse for her father's actions against the new king, Joffrey. It didn't work, but she still tried it. For a place like Westeros, full of violence and brutality, a powerful painkiller would be a very valuable commodity. Almost as valuable as knowing how to make it yourself.

Wildfire

2 ounces pear vodka
1 ounce apple pucker
½ ounce lime juice
A barspoon of melon liqueur
A barspoon of blue curaçao

Pour all ingredients into a
shaker. Shake and strain into
a chilled martini glass.

OPTIONAL: Float a layer of high
proof rum, such as Bacardi 151, on the top
of the finished drink. Light it on fire for effect
but remember to very carefully blow out the
fire before drinking it. Seriously.

It is known by a few names:
"pyromancer's piss," "the substance,"
or as we know it best, wildfire. It is
the vibrant green, super flammable
liquid death cooked up by the
Alchemists' Guild in King's Landing.
Once ignited, wildfire has a green
flame and is said to "burn so hot it
melts wood, stone, even steel. And,
of course, flesh." Wildfire is how
Tyrion Lannister almost completely
destroyed Stannis Baratheon's entire
navy in one move. Jaime Lannister
killed "The Mad King" because he
was going to burn his whole city
and all of the people in it with wildfire. Also,
Aerion Targaryen thought drinking wildfire
would turn him into a dragon. Sadly, it didn't
work out for him. In *Game of Thrones*, wildfire
is an extremely powerful recipe with incredible
destructive potential. In this book, it is a very
delicious alcoholic crowd-pleaser. It won't burn
you or turn you into a dragon, but it will give
you a pretty good buzz.

THE WALKING DEAD

Atlanta Zombie

1 ounce honey syrup
1 ounce dark rum
1 ounce gold rum
½ ounce lemon juice
2 ounces peach puree
A few drops of grenadine syrup

To make the honey syrup, simply mix 1 part honey to 2 parts warm water and stir until the honey is dissolved.

PUREE

To make the peach puree, in a blender, add two peaches, peeled and with stone removed, one barspoon of grenadine, and 2 ounces of water. Blend until smooth and refrigerate before using.

Combine all ingredients except grenadine in a shaker with ice. Shake and strain into a Collins glass full of ice cubes. Drip the grenadine on the top of the drink and garnish with a piece of peach.

Imagine getting shot while on the job and slipping into a coma only to wake a few weeks later, and everyone is dead. Well, undead rather. They also look horribly rotted and are trying desperately to eat you. This is what happened to Atlanta police officer Rick Grimes (Andrew Lincoln). This instant classic horror-drama made its television debut on Halloween 2010. Originally The Walking Dead was a series of graphic novels, and it was already a fan obsession before the first episode ever aired. The story is centered in the southeastern United States, starting in Atlanta, Georgia, and moving around other areas in the same region. In this grim vision of the near future, the thousands of flesh-eating zombies everywhere are not the only problem. The remaining people left on the planet have become anarchic and violent in their various attempts at survival in this chaotic new world. This drink is made with peaches, because the story starts in Georgia. Georgia is known for it's great peaches, so much so that is called "The Peach State." Another thing: This drink looks fleshy in color and a little bloody with the dripped grenadine. Kind of gross looking, but it is actually very delicious.

LIQUOR INDEX

The problem with the world is
that everyone is a few drinks behind.

— HUMPHREY BOGART

ABOUT THE CONTRIBUTORS

ANTHONY MARINESE is a noted bartender who has scoured the trendiest bars in San Francisco before recently moving to the East Coast.

Born in Uruguay, **HORACIO COSSINELLI** graduated from the School of Fine Arts in Paris. After years serving major international brands, he decided to focus exclusively on painting and illustration.

Special Thanks

Thanks to Trax Bar and all my friends and regulars. Thanks to Rodolphe, Raj, Horacio, and Stephanie. Thanks to San Francisco, and thanks to New York City.

—Anthony

I especially want to thank Enrique, James, Paul, and Toni for their help throughout this project, and Anthony and Rodolphe in their different time zone.

—Horacio

INSIGHT EDITIONS

PO Box 3088
San Rafael, CA 94912
www.insighteditions.com

 Find us on Facebook: www.facebook.com/InsightEditions

 Follow us on Twitter: @insighteditions

First published in the United States in 2016 by Insight Editions.
Originally published in France in 2015
by ©2015 HUGINN&MUNINN / Mediatoon Licensing.

Library of Congress Cataloging-in-Publication Data available.

ISBN: 978-1-60887-859-8

ROOTS of PEACE   REPLANTED PAPER

Insight Editions, in association with Roots of Peace, will plant two trees for each tree used in the manufacturing of this book. Roots of Peace is an internationally renowned humanitarian organization dedicated to eradicating land mines worldwide and converting war-torn lands into productive farms and wildlife habitats. Roots of Peace will plant two million fruit and nut trees in Afghanistan and provide farmers there with the skills and support necessary for sustainable land use.

Manufactured in China by Insight Editions

10 9 8 7 6 5 4 3 2 1